A Children's Museum
Activity Book

BALL-POINT PENS

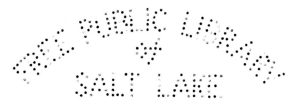
A Children's Museum Activity Book

BALL-POINT PENS

by Bernie Zubrowski

Illustrated by Linda Bourke

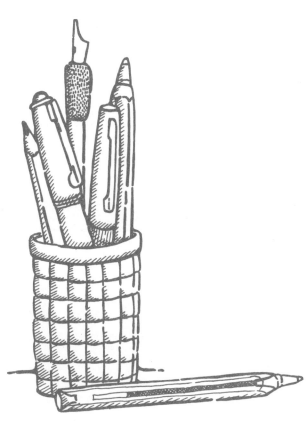

Little, Brown and Company

Boston　　Toronto

Children's Museum Activity Books in This Series

BUBBLES
BALL-POINT PENS
MILK CARTON BLOCKS

COPYRIGHT © 1979 BY THE CHILDREN'S MUSEUM

FIRST EDITION

Library of Congress Cataloging in Publication Data

Zubrowski, Bernie.

    A Children's Museum activity book: Ball-point pens.
    SUMMARY: Explains how a ball-point pen works. Presents directions for constructing tools and devices with parts of pens and for using them in experiments and demonstrations.
    1. Physics — Experiments — Juvenile literature.
2. Ball-point pens — Juvenile literature. [1. Physics —Experiments. 2. Experiments. 3. Ball-point pens] I. Bourke, Linda. II. Title. III. Series: Boston. Children's Museum. A Children's Museum activity book.
QC26.Z82   530'.028   78-31622
ISBN 0-316-98882-0
ISBN 0-316-98883-9 pbk.

Published simultaneously in Canada
by Little, Brown & Company (Canada) Limited

PRINTED IN THE UNITED STATES OF AMERICA

INTRODUCTION

A ball-point pen is more complicated than it looks. It is much more than a tube with a ball bearing at the end of it. Its tip is designed especially to take advantage of certain properties of liquids. The ink is not just colored water, but a liquid selected for qualities that result in uniform writing.

Additionally, a ball-point pen can be more than an instrument for writing. By taking it apart, you can construct other tools: a balance, an eyedropper, a thermometer, or a prism. And these are only the beginning.

Tools made from parts of ball-point pens can be used in experiments that will help you learn how pens work. With the balance you make you can weigh the ink, for instance, or test how sticky it is. The following pages suggest further experiments, and give instructions on how to make other useful and fun devices with parts of the ball-point pen.

When I was initially devising these experiments, I used a Bic pen. This is especially useful because it has a clear plastic barrel. For many of the experiments, however, other brands such as Great Western or Write Bros. would work equally well.

LOOKING CLOSELY AT THE PEN

It may seem that the operation of the pen is very simple. Ink just flows down the tube to the ball, and the ball rolls it onto the paper. This is essentially true, but the ink is a special kind of liquid, and the tip is especially designed to make sure the ink goes onto the paper evenly.

The idea behind the pen may be simple, but putting it into practice is not. Inventors had envisioned some sort of ball-point pen more than eighty years ago, but although there were a number of attempts to make one, none of them worked very well. It took a Hungarian sculptor, Lázló Biró and his brother George, a chemist, to come up with the right combination of a good design and an ink that wouldn't leak out of the pen.

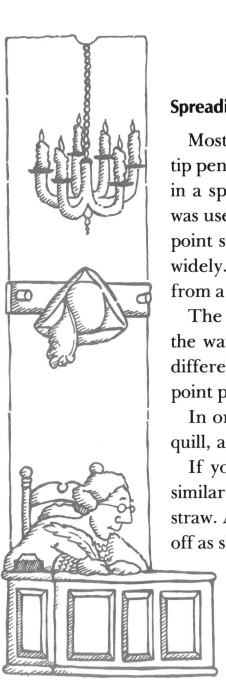

Spreading the Ink

Most pens used today are either ball-point or felt-tip pens. Each type of pen puts the ink onto the paper in a special way. Not too long ago the fountain pen was used a great deal. The nib pen, which has a metal point similar to that of a fountain pen, was also used widely. Earlier in history people used a quill made from a reed or feather for writing.

The fountain pen, nib pen and quill are similar in the way they place ink on the paper. There are big differences, however, between the workings of a ball-point pen and a fountain pen or quill.

In order to see these differences try writing with a quill, a nib pen, a fountain pen and a ball-point pen.

If you don't have a feather, you can make a pen similar to a quill by cutting off the end of a drinking straw. A small-diameter straw works best. Cut the end off as shown in the drawing. Don't make the angle too

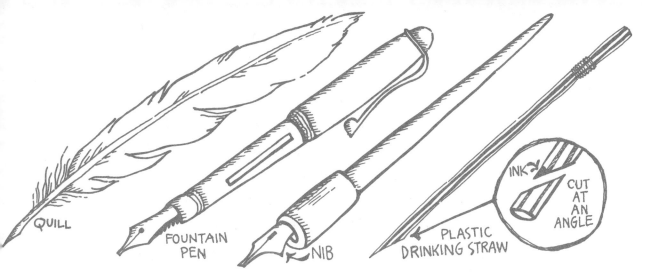

QUILL

FOUNTAIN
PEN

NIB

PLASTIC
DRINKING STRAW

INK

CUT
AT
AN
ANGLE

sharp. For ink, one can use food color or any other colored substance that dissolves in water.

Dip the pointed end into the food color. It will take a little practice to move the point across the paper and get even writing. Watch closely how the ink goes from the tip of the straw to the paper. How many words can you write before you run out of ink?

Next, try to get a fountain pen. Perhaps there are some old ones lying around a desk drawer in your house. If not, some stores still sell them, as well as the kind of pen that uses a nib. A nib is the pointed metal part of the pen that is attached to a wooden shaft.

Try writing with a fountain pen to see how it works. How does the ink get from the tube holding the ink to the tip of the pen without flowing all over the paper? The fountain pen has one definite advantage over the feather-type pen. With a fountain pen you can write many words before you have to refill the pen with more ink.

To see how the ink gets from the tube to the paper in a ball-point pen is difficult since the ball is very small and the tip is covered. Here is a device which can help you understand how it works. Cut off the tip of a plastic dishwashing soap bottle. (Check the drawing for exactly where to cut.) Find a marble which fits

HOW MANY WORDS CAN YOU WRITE WITH ONE DIP WITH A QUILL?

FOUNTAIN PENS WRITE MANY WORDS BEFORE NEEDING A REFILL.

INK

snugly in the hole you have made in the tip. It doesn't have to go inside the hole, but must be large enough to cover the hole. This makes something like a large ball-point pen.

Get some paper. Put the marble on the paper. Then place the hole of the bottle on top of the marble. Put a tablespoon of water and food color inside and start writing. Try any colored liquids you have around. You could try making thick ink by mixing syrup and food color. How does this pen write with a thin liquid?

How does it write with a thick liquid such as syrup? Which type of liquid spreads best on the paper; which dries the quickest?

In making your own ball-point, you may find either that the liquid leaks around the marble or that it is spread on the paper in an uneven manner. These are the same kinds of problems that bothered those who first attempted to make a ball-point pen a long time ago.

THE WEIGHT OF THE INK

If you try writing with a ball-point pen upside down, you find that soon it will no longer write. Turn it back to its normal position and it will write again. It seems that the weight of the liquid keeps it in contact with the ball so that the ball can spread it on the paper. Does this mean the ink has to be a very heavy liquid? How does the heaviness of the ink compare to that of other common liquids?

There are several ways of comparing weights of liquids. The most obvious way is with a balance, and the following pages show how to assemble a balance from parts of ball-point pens.

An Equal-Arm Balance

Balances can be made from all sorts of materials, but it is particularly hard to make one that will weigh small quantities of materials accurately. Here is a design for one that can be quickly assembled.

YOU WILL NEED:
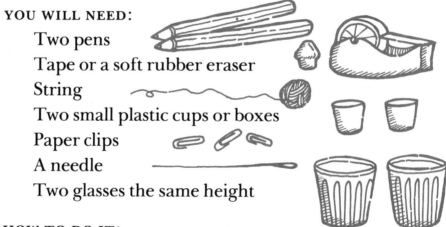
Two pens
Tape or a soft rubber eraser
String
Two small plastic cups or boxes
Paper clips
A needle
Two glasses the same height

HOW TO DO IT:

1. The two pens can be joined together with tape or with a rubber eraser.

2. Place the needle through the tape or rubber eraser, making sure it is the same distance from the ends of the two pens.

3. Tie the two plastic cups or boxes to the end of each pen. The inner tube of each pen can be pulled out and then reinserted with the string from the cups wrapped around the tip of the pen. In this manner, the cups are secured.

4. Paper clips can be used as weights.

CUT

USE MASKING TAPE OR HOLLOW TUBE CUT FROM ERASER TO JOIN PENS

WEIGH 20 BARRELS
OF WATER IN PAPER
CLIPS, THEN COMPARE
WITH SYRUP, OIL, ETC.

Using this balance, and the capped outer tube of a pen as a measure of volume, you can determine the relative weights of different liquids. One way to do this is to measure out a definite amount of liquid and see how much this liquid weighs in paper clips. For instance, fill the barrel of the pen twenty times, each time emptying the liquid into one bucket of the balance. After the twentieth time, add paper clips to the other bucket until it balances.

In this manner, one can find out how many paper clips it takes to balance twenty barrels full of water. How many clips are needed to balance the same amount of food color? Try comparing the following liquids: water, food color, salt water, alcohol, nail polish remover, syrup, and oil. Which is the heaviest and which is the lightest?

You can use another ball-point pen tool to check the results of your weighing: a hydrometer.

HYDROMETER

Sometimes it is useful to know whether some liquid is heavier than another, or how much of a solid, such as sugar or salt, has been dissolved in the water. An instrument that can answer questions like these is called a hydrometer. Basically, it is a sealed cylinder that floats vertically in liquid. It will float at different levels depending on how dense the liquid is. Using the ink tube of a ball-point pen, you can easily make one.

YOU WILL NEED:

The ink tube of a pen with the plastic, ball-point tip

Straight pins

If there is any ink left in the tube, clean it out. This may require some patience. First take off the plastic

CLEANING THE PENS

CAREFULLY BLOW OUT INK.

SAVE INK TO USE LATER.

BOTTLE TOP — TIP

NEW POLISH OFF — ALCOHOL

SOAK TIP IN POLISH REMOVER →

POUR ALCOHOL OR NAIL POLISH REMOVER THROUGH TUBE TILL CLEAN.

HYDROMETER

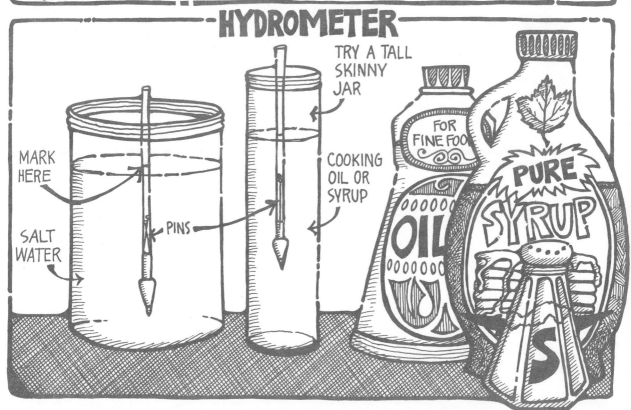

MARK HERE

SALT WATER

PINS

TRY A TALL SKINNY JAR

COOKING OIL OR SYRUP

FOR FINE FOOD

OIL

PURE SYRUP

tip and blow the ink out of the tube into a small container like a bottle top. Save it for use later. Then pour alcohol, or better yet, nail polish remover, through the tube until all the ink residue is dissolved. You can clean the plastic tip by soaking it in a small amount of nail polish remover in a paper cup.

Place the writing tip back onto the tube and float it in the water. You may have to put a couple of pins into the tube to get it floating upright. You can mark the tube to show how great a length is floating above the surface of the water, or you can simply measure this length with a ruler.

Use your hydrometer in a tall, skinny jar or glass. You can fill this jar with different liquids, such as salt water, syrup or cooking oil. You will find that the tube will float at different heights in different liquids. The heavier the liquid, the more of the tube will float above it.

OIL WILL FLOAT

WATER

HEAVIER
LIQUIDS
WILL SINK.

Test the liquids you weighed with your equal-arm balance, and record the results.

As yet, you haven't been able to determine the relative weight of the ink in a ball-point pen. This has been hard to do since there isn't enough ink in the pen to weigh accurately, or to fill a jar to test with the hydrometer. But now that you have found some order in the weights of liquids, you can perform one quick, simple test that will give you some idea of how heavy the ink is.

First, add a drop of the different liquids you have tested to water. You will find that those that are heavier than water will sink. Those that are lighter, such as oil, will float.

Now try dropping ball-point-pen ink into each of these different liquids. In which does it sink? In which does it float?

How does the weight of ink compare to syrup? To water?

INK FROM PEN

SYRUP   OIL   SALT WATER

IN WHICH DOES
THE INK SINK?

An Eyedropper

The above experiments sometimes require you to measure liquids by the drop. If you don't have an eyedropper handy, you can easily improvise one from the outer barrel of a pen.

YOU WILL NEED:

Barrel of a ball-point pen
Drinking straw that fits into the barrel
Tape

HOW TO DO IT:

1. Take out the inner tube and end plug of the pen.
2. Tape the hole, if there is one, on the side of the barrel.
3. Fit the drinking straw snugly inside the barrel.

4. Fold the remaining end of the straw over twice, so that the end is well sealed.

Place the barrel in water. Squeeze the straw with several fingers so that air bubbles come out. If air bubbles don't come, the straw may not be sealed tightly into the barrel, or the tape may be loose. Release your grip on the straw while the barrel is still in the water, and the water should rise into the barrel. Then, by squeezing the straw lightly, you can measure out the water a drop at a time.

SQUEEZE HERE, THEN RELEASE TO FILL BARREL →

STRAW SHOULD FIT SNUGLY

TAPE HOLE

WATER

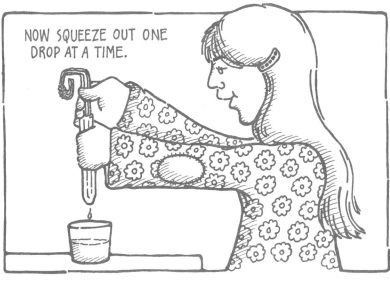

NOW SQUEEZE OUT ONE DROP AT A TIME.

THE STICKINESS OR COHESIVENESS OF LIQUIDS

Related to the thickness of the ink or other liquids is its stickiness, or how well it holds together. This is an important property especially for the ink in a ball-point pen. For instance, if you were to drop the pen onto the floor, the ink would break up in the tube if it didn't hold together very well. Nor would it flow smoothly to the ball—the writing would be uneven. Using the equal-arm balance, you can measure the cohesiveness of liquids.

YOU WILL NEED:

An equal-arm balance like the one described earlier

The plastic top from a yogurt or ice cream container

String

Paper clips

HOW TO DO IT:

1. Set up the balance as shown at right.

2. From the plastic container top, cut a square about an inch on a side.

3. Tape four pieces of string to it, making sure none of the string hangs over the side.

4. Hang it on the balance.

5. Balance the plastic square with a few paper clips before putting it on top of the liquid.

6. Carefully put the plastic onto the surface of the liquid, making sure it sits just on the surface.

7. Slowly add paper clips to the bucket until the square is pulled off the liquid.

8. Wipe off the plastic very well. Then do the same procedure with other liquids.

As you are adding the paper clips, put them into the cup carefully, trying not to jar the balance. Be

CUT A 1-INCH
SQUARE

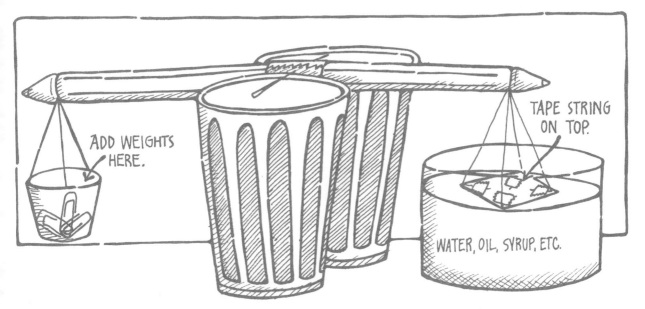

ADD WEIGHTS HERE.

TAPE STRING ON TOP.

WATER, OIL, SYRUP, ETC.

especially careful when it looks as if the plastic is just about to come off. Watch closely at the point when the plate is about to come off. You should be able to see the plate pulling the liquid, showing that what you are measuring is how strongly the liquid is keeping itself together.

Compare the stickiness of those liquids you have previously investigated: cooking oil, alcohol, salt water, syrup. Which takes the most paper clips to pull the plastic off? Which takes the fewest?

RECORD YOUR FINDINGS

STICKINESS OF LIQUIDS

LIQUID	CLIPS
SALT WATER	3-4
ALCOHOL	
NAIL POLISH REMOVER	
OIL	

If you have several ball-point pens around, you could try getting ink from each of these and measuring the stickiness of ink from each one. One further experiment you could try is to see what difference it makes if a smaller piece or bigger piece of plastic is used. Does the size of the plastic make a difference in how many paper clips you need to pull it off the liquid?

Capillary Attraction

When Lázló Biró invented the ball-point pen, he decided to have the ink feed to the ball through a small tube as shown in the diagram. You would think this is the opposite of what needs to be done. In most situations, smaller tubes slow down liquids. Biró was taking advantage of a special property of liquids. Liquids have a tendency to creep into small spaces, and this is called *capillarity*. Here is a way to see this for yourself.

YOU WILL NEED:

Two ball-point pens with clear barrels.

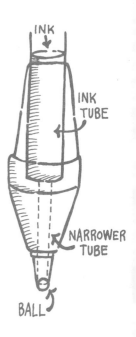

INK

INK TUBE

NARROWER TUBE

BALL

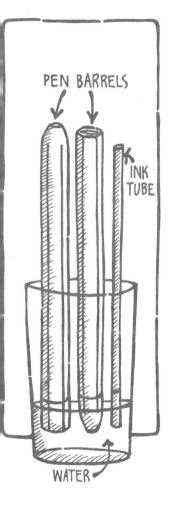

PEN BARRELS

INK TUBE

WATER

HOW TO DO IT:

1. Clean two barrels and one ink tube from the ball-point pens very thoroughly.

2. Now dip opposite ends of the barrels, and a tube into clean water as shown. If you look very carefully at the parts touching the water, you will find that water has crept up the tubes. The narrower the tube, the higher it creeps up. Does it seem that one end of a barrel is narrower than the other?

This type of action can be further demonstrated with the water rising even higher. Here we can use the same clear barrels as test tubes.

Fill several tubes or barrels with different kinds of clay, dirt, sawdust, and chalk dust as shown in the drawing. Place these tubes in an inch or so of water in a jar and then watch carefully. Adding food color to the water can make it more visible as it moves up the barrel. Does the water rise at the same rate in all the tubes? Is there a difference in the rate of rise between a tube containing coarse sand and one containing fine sand?

If you can get some powdered clay, compare the rates of the rising with the same clay packed loosely and tightly in different tubes. In which tube will the water rise the highest? In all these situations is there any relationship between how fast and how far up the water will travel, and the size of the spaces between the particles in the tubes?

Having seen the action of water in small spaces, you can now see why Biró made a small tube near the tip of his pen. In this way the ball is always kept moistened by capillary attraction.

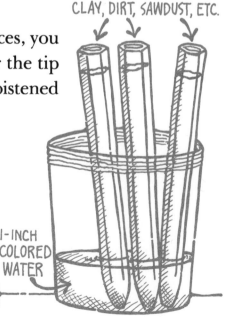

CLAY, DIRT, SAWDUST, ETC.

FOOD COLOR

1-INCH COLORED WATER

Drying the Ink

When you write with a fountain pen or a drinking-straw pen, the ink flows thickly onto the paper. It takes a while to dry. With a ball-point or felt-tip pen, you can wipe your hand over the writing as soon as it is placed on the paper without smearing it. How does the ink dry in each situation? Is the rate of drying determined more by how quickly the liquid evaporates into the air, or by how much of it is absorbed into the paper?

One way of seeing how quickly liquids dry is to set up the following experiment. Into small bottle caps or containers, place equal quantities of liquids and inks. You can use a ball-point-pen eyedropper to do this.

Check the level of each in a few hours and then the next day. You should find that some of the liquids such as alcohol and nail polish remover disappear very quickly, while others are still in the caps the next day.

In fact, the ink from the ball-point pen hasn't gone into the air at all!

The ink in felt-tip pens is a combination of dyes and a liquid which is similar to nail polish remover. Once placed on the paper it is absorbed very quickly by the paper and also evaporates speedily.

Ink in fountain pens is mostly water, and you have seen that water takes a while to evaporate. Therefore, when placed on paper, fountain pen ink takes a while to dry.

The ink in a ball-point pen is placed very thinly on the paper. It is absorbed by the paper, but the ink also forms a skin when it comes into contact with the air. You may have noticed this when you examined the cap holding the ink the next day. This skin keeps the ink from smearing.

SOME CONCLUSIONS

If you have done all the investigations on the preceding pages, and watched closely what happened in each situation, you have developed an understanding of how complex a ball-point pen is. If you put all this information together you could describe how a ball-point pen works.

The ball-point pen won't write upside down because the weight of the ink will pull it away from the ball. In order for the pen to work, the ink must move down the tube to the ball. The thickness of the ink helps in two ways. First, when the pen is dropped, the liquid won't break up in the tube. Second, the combination of the thickness and the property of capillary attraction helps the ball bearing deliver ink to the paper in a continuous, uniform way.

THE COLOR OF INK

On some pens it will say that the ink is washable while on others it will say that it is permanent. Can the ink from a ball-point pen be washed off with water? If not, what other kinds of liquids might you try to get ink off clothes or erase it from paper?

Try dipping cloth or paper with ink on it into the following liquids: water, soapy water, alcohol, Lestoil, Mr. Clean, bleach, or any other cleaning agent you have around the house. Let your samples dry overnight.

While waiting for the results, here is a quick test which will give you some indication of what will happen with these liquids. Rub ink from the pen in small areas on absorbent paper such as a paper towel. Carefully add drops of one of the liquids to this ink spot. Do this several times and wait a few minutes for results. What happens to ink spots treated with different liquids?

In which situation would you say the liquid has mixed with the ink?

Will you get the same sort of spreading if you add these liquids to a food color dropped on paper?

Try different kinds of felt-tip pens. Some of these are labeled "permanent and waterproof." Does that mean that no liquids will remove this ink from paper?

If you look carefully at some of the spreading circles of ink mixed with other fluids, you will see that what was once black ink is now a mixture of blue and other colors. It happens that many inks are not pure colors but mixtures of several. To see if inks in ball-point pens are mixtures and to determine how many colors are in the mixtures, you can set up the following apparatus.

SOAPY WATER

BLEACH AAA

TRY LESTOIL, MR. CLEAN, ETC.

INK SPOTS

PAPER TOWEL

A clear bottle or jar
White paper towel
Water
Alcohol
Nail polish remover

HOW TO DO IT:

1. Put some water into the bottom of the bottle.

2. Dab some ink from a ball-point or felt-tip pen onto a strip of paper towel, and hang this strip from the side of the bottle. Do not immerse the ink spot in the water, but let the bottom of the strip of paper touch the water so that the liquid can slowly creep up to the ink spot. Notice what happens to the ink when the water reaches it.

3. Try different types of ink on separate paper

towels, and compare the results. Try alcohol and nail polish remover in place of the water.

Does the same ink separate in the same way when different liquids are used on it? Is the blue color from a ball-point pen, from a felt-tip pen, and from a drop of blue food color affected in the same way by the same liquid?

Having tried all of the above activities, which liquid would you use to clean blue ink from a piece of cloth? Which liquid would you use to erase ball-point-pen ink from paper?

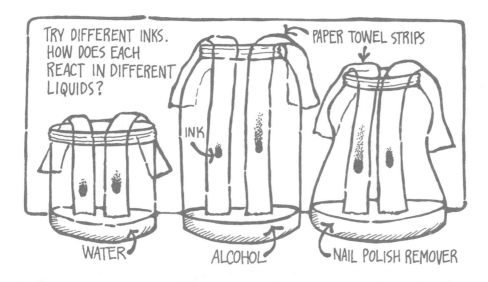

TRY DIFFERENT INKS. HOW DOES EACH REACT IN DIFFERENT LIQUIDS?

PAPER TOWEL STRIPS

INK

WATER

ALCOHOL

NAIL POLISH REMOVER

INVESTIGATING OTHER PARTS OF THE PEN

There are three different kinds of plastic in the makeup of a ball-point pen. This is because of the special properties of each plastic. There are several advantages in using plastics. Generally they are light, and very strong for their weight. They can be easily molded into many different shapes. They also are not destroyed easily by chemicals.

Let us take a look at how strong some plastics are. How does a ball-point pen compare to a pencil, or other kinds of pens in strength? Some pencils are thicker than the plastic barrel. Does that mean the pencil is stronger? Here is one way you could test the strength of pens or pencils.

Try to find some pieces of thick wood that you can put across a deep sink or bathtub. The wood should be about twelve centimeters apart. Put a pen across the gap between the pieces of wood. Hang a bucket from the pen. The bucket should not touch the bottom of the tub.

Gradually add water to the bucket. Do this until the pen breaks. Be careful; sometimes the broken pieces may jump a little into the air when it breaks.

Measure the amount of water it took to break the pen. This can be done in one way by measuring the depth of the water with a ruler. Then try the same experiment with a pencil. Which is stronger?

MEASURING STRENGTH

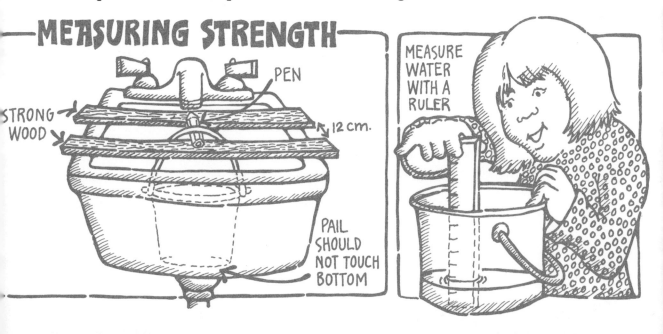

PEN

STRONG WOOD

12 cm.

PAIL SHOULD NOT TOUCH BOTTOM

MEASURE WATER WITH A RULER

THE OUTER TUBE

Many things today are designed in such a way that they not only function well but also are pleasing in appearance. The transparent barrel of a Bic pen is both functional and visually pleasing. It is strong and enables us to see how much ink is left. It does not roll around because of the flat surfaces, and at the same time it produces interesting effects with light.

Consider how this barrel interacts with light. Hold it up to allow strong light to pass through it, and move it in various ways. Place it on a page of print and look at the letters through the tube. For comparison, do the same with a transparent tube that is round. While playing around, here are some questions to consider and experiments to try.

Place a pen on a page of print. Are you able to see parts of letters which are just below the body of the pen? Why are you able to do this even though there is an inner tube of ink preventing a direct view?

Take out the ink tube. Place the barrel on a line of print. How many times can you see the same word when looking through the barrel?

Light travels in a straight line. It can be bent by materials, and concentrated as with a lens. With the inner tube removed from the pen, play around and note what happens to strong light such as sunlight as you move the barrel up and down or twist it a few inches above the paper. How does the shadow it casts change as you move the barrel from the paper, to one, two, and three inches above the paper? Can you produce any bright areas directly beneath the tube? Any dark areas?

As you were moving the barrel around, you may have noticed flashes of color. If you line it up with the

BRIGHT LIGHT

PAPER

WHAT HAPPENS
WHEN YOU TWIST
AND MOVE THE
PEN BARREL?

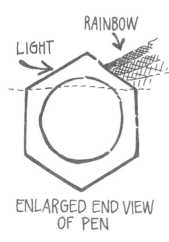

RAINBOW

LIGHT

ENLARGED END VIEW
OF PEN

direction of the light in a certain way, you can produce a rainbow or spectrum of colors. How many colors are there? Are these colors like the color you see in a rainbow or a soap film?

The Bic tube can be thought of as being composed of several triangles. Such triangular solid shapes are called *prisms*, and when light travels through them at a certain angle, a rainbow is projected.

Try to get papers of different colors such as construction paper. Make a rainbow again; this time shine it on the papers of different colors. What happens when the rainbow falls on red paper? Can you see all other colors of the rainbow, or have they changed in some way? What happens if rainbows fall on dark blue paper, or black paper?

If water or some other liquid is placed inside the barrel, does it make any difference in the appearance of the rainbow?

Find a transparent tube shaped like a cylinder. Try to make a rainbow with this. Unless this tube is very thick, you won't be able to produce any color.

Another Way of Bending Light

You discovered that light can be bent by the barrel. The hexagonal shape caused this result. What would happen if you were to change the shape in some way? Suppose a drop of water were placed on one side? We would then have a partly cylindrical shape.

With the ink tube still out, and the barrel lying on a piece of newspaper, put a small round drop of water on the barrel as shown in the diagram. Look through this drop at the words on the newspaper. Has the drop on the barrel changed the words in any way? Put other thin objects such as a wire inside the barrel, and look at them through the water drop. Do they look any different when viewed through a water drop?

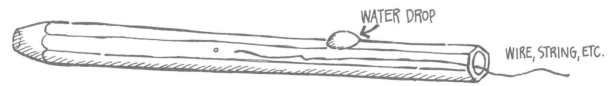

WATER DROP

WIRE, STRING, ETC.

Now, is it the combination of the barrel and the round drop that is magnifying the letters, or is it the drop itself? Here is one way of finding out.

With a hacksaw, carefully cut off a very small cross section of the outer tube. The slice should be no more than two or three millimeters thick. Smooth the surface of both sides of this slice so that no burrs remain. Put a wire around the slice as shown in the drawing.

With a matchstick or toothpick, carefully put a drop of water into the hole of the slice, as shown in the diagram. Look through the drop at the page of a book or newspaper.

Then put another drop of water into the hole. Look at the page again. Does it look different from the way it did when only a little water was in the hole?

You now have made a small magnifier. It can be used to look at small objects, or at insects.

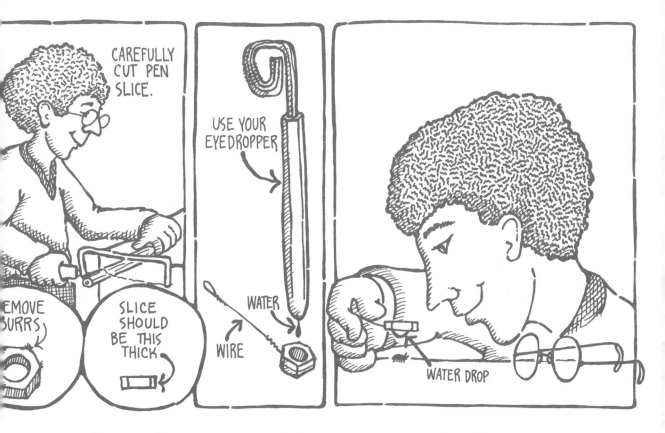

If you take away some of the water, you may be able to get a drop of water that makes things look smaller than they really are. If you wear glasses, see if there is a position closer to you where you can see clearly through it when you take off your glasses.

OTHER DEVICES

On the preceding pages you not only had a chance to learn how a ball-point pen works, but along the way also saw how it can be converted into useful instruments with which you can do experiments. So far, there have been directions for making a balance, hydrometer, eyedropper, prism, and magnifier. You can make other devices that will help in doing other kinds of experiments. The following pages show you how to make these.

A Ball-Point-Pen Thermometer

The results you get with this may not be as accurate as those from a store-bought thermometer, but it will work, and tell you the relative heat and coldness of different liquids.

One transparent ball-point pen
Nail polish remover or alcohol (for cleaning)
Tape
Clay or gum
Food color

HOW TO DO IT:

1. Remove the writing tip and clean the ink tube, according to the instructions given on pages 17–19.

2. Tape the hole on the side of the pen. Seal the bottom part with the cap as well as with some clay or gum to make sure no air will leak out this end.

3. Put a small slug of colored water about a quarter-inch long into the ink tube. Put this into the barrel slowly, then seal the other end with some clay also.

THERMOMETER

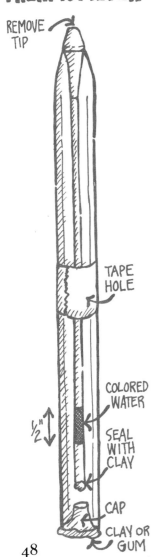

REMOVE TIP

TAPE HOLE

COLORED WATER

SEAL WITH CLAY

½"

CAP

CLAY OR GUM

There are a number of activities you can try with this thermometer. Here are some suggestions:

First of all, place the tube three quarters of the way into a glass of hot water you have obtained from a faucet. Watch the slug of water in the tube. If the tube is sealed properly, the water should rise up the tube. If the water is very hot in the glass, the slug may go all the way to the top.

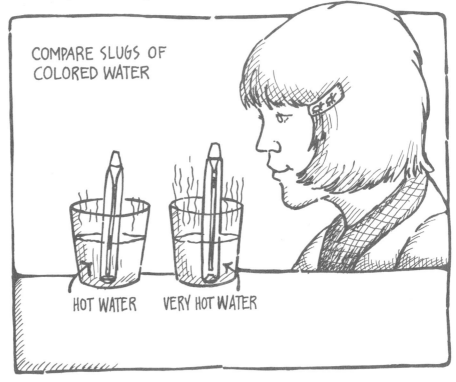

COMPARE SLUGS OF COLORED WATER

HOT WATER   VERY HOT WATER

48

What happens when the half-inch of water is placed in different parts of the tube as in the following arrangement?

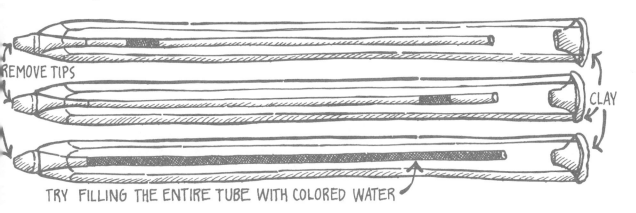

REMOVE TIPS

CLAY

TRY FILLING THE ENTIRE TUBE WITH COLORED WATER

Another experiment you can try is to use two thermometers to compare the cooling rates of hot water in different kinds of containers. For instance, which cools faster: hot water in a Styrofoam cup or in a plastic cup? Remember to use the same amount of water and to fill both with hot water from the faucet at the same time.

A Short-Interval Timer

Most clocks give us the time in hours and minutes. A second hand on some clocks can help us measure intervals in seconds. Using the barrel of a pen, one can make a clock that measures intervals of five, ten, and fifteen seconds.

YOU WILL NEED:

One pen that is transparent, with the inner tube removed

Clay or gum

Transparent tape

Soapy water or alcohol

HOW TO DO IT:

1. Remove the ink tube and cap. Remove the writing tip from the ink tube, and clean the ink from all parts.

2. Place clay into the writing tip and into the small cap that fits into the other end of the barrel.

3. Put the barrel into a container of soapy water, taking care not to make lots of bubbles inside the tube. If you use alcohol instead of soapy water, the problem of bubbles won't arise.

4. With the barrel still in the water, put the tip into the barrel. Then take the barrel out of the water.

5. Remove just a little liquid from the tube to make an air gap as shown. Put the cap back on.

Now you will have to do some fiddling around. Starting with a certain size air bubble, time how long it takes to get from one end of the tube to the other when the tube is held upside down and vertically.

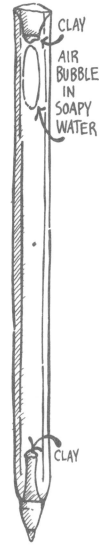

CLAY

AIR BUBBLE IN SOAPY WATER

CLAY

HOW LONG DOES IT TAKE FOR THE BUBBLE TO RISE?

Depending on the size of the air bubble, the time can be from three to twenty seconds. Can you adjust the size of the air bubble so that it takes five seconds?

Note: The insides of some barrels are not even (those of Bic pens, for example). A bubble will take a longer time going toward the ball bearing than the other way. So, always time bubbles rising in the same direction.

A Paint Brush or Filter-Tip Pen

A ball-point pen can be easily changed into something similar to a felt-tip pen. Just take out the inner tube and end plug, and tape the hole on the side. Cut a piece of unused cigarette filter and place it into the barrel so that it fits snugly. Then with your ball-point-pen eyedropper carefully add food color as shown. Replace the end plug; let the food color soak through the filter; then start writing. Placing the barrel in a horizontal position will stop the liquid from flowing.

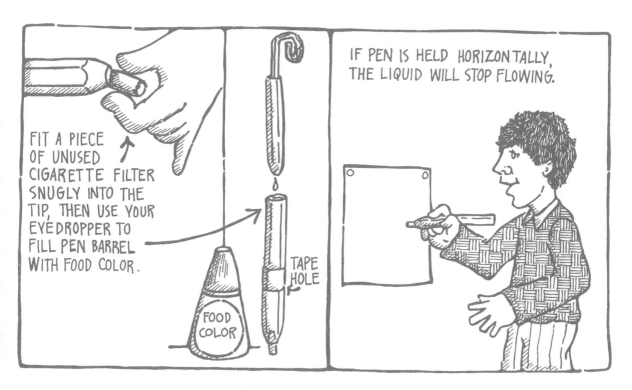

FIT A PIECE OF UNUSED CIGARETTE FILTER SNUGLY INTO THE TIP, THEN USE YOUR EYEDROPPER TO FILL PEN BARREL WITH FOOD COLOR.

FOOD COLOR

TAPE HOLE

IF PEN IS HELD HORIZONTALLY, THE LIQUID WILL STOP FLOWING.

The Ball-Point Pen as a Measuring Tool

Occasionally we need to measure something, but a ruler for measuring length or a cup for measuring volume isn't around. More than likely, we will be carrying a ball-point pen with us. Why not use this as our measuring instrument? With a little memorization we will be ready to measure any small thing.

In addition, it is sometimes difficult to appreciate or have a feeling for a unit of measurement. We see the unit "millimeter" on a ruler, but what everyday object is a millimeter? It so happens that the diameter of the ball of a medium Bic pen is a millimeter. This same ball weighs seven milligrams. Also, the idea of cubic centimeters may still seem rather foreign to Americans; just look at the inner tube of a Bic pen. It holds close to a cubic centimeter when filled.

So, for future reference here are some measurements of a Bic pen and its parts.

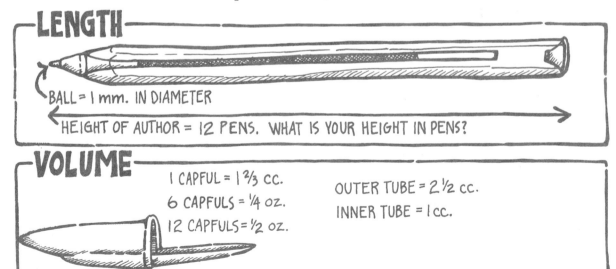

LENGTH

BALL = 1 mm. IN DIAMETER

HEIGHT OF AUTHOR = 12 PENS. WHAT IS YOUR HEIGHT IN PENS?

VOLUME

1 CAPFUL = 1⅔ cc.
6 CAPFULS = ¼ oz.
12 CAPFULS = ½ oz.

OUTER TUBE = 2½ cc.
INNER TUBE = 1 cc.

FURTHER ADVENTURES WITH BALL-POINT PENS

There are lots of ways of using the pen and its parts, as you can see. Many investigations can be carried out using them. On the next few pages are more devices that can be made from the pen. Each is a fun toy to play with, but each also demonstrates something about scientific principles. So, read on, make the toys, and explore with them.

A Pen That Writes on Water

You have probably seen skywriting. A pilot in a plane draws letters in the sky with a special kind of smoke. The letters gradually change their shape. Eventually, the smoke is blown away.

Somewhat similar to skywriting is water-writing. By changing a ball-point pen and adding a balloon, one can make a pen that writes on water. This device will also help you observe tiny bubbles and their interaction.

A medium-size balloon
About two feet of string
A clean ink tube
Masking tape
A large shallow tray such as a cookie tray
A rubber band

HOW TO DO IT:

1. Pull out inner part of pen with pliers and take off the tip. If you don't already have an empty pen, remove the ink and clean the parts.
2. Remove the metal tip from the gold, plastic nose-cone.
3. With a pin and pliers, force out the small ball in the writing tip.

4. Soak all parts of the tip in alcohol to make sure each is clean of ink.

5. Put the small metal part back into the gold plastic.

6. Put the cleaned ink tube into this.

7. Fill a pan with soapy water. You are now ready to make small bubbles on the water.

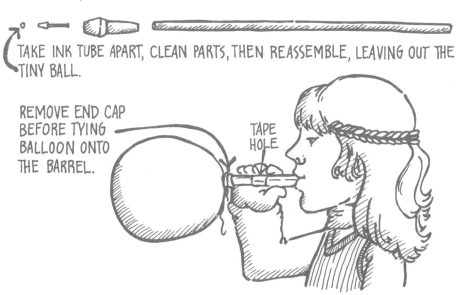

TAKE INK TUBE APART, CLEAN PARTS, THEN REASSEMBLE, LEAVING OUT THE TINY BALL.

REMOVE END CAP BEFORE TYING BALLOON ONTO THE BARREL.

TAPE HOLE

8. With the rubber band, attach the balloon to the back end of the pen.

9. With the inner tube removed, blow up the balloon until it is large.

10. Quickly put the inner tube back into the main body of the pen.

11. Then, with the tip of the pen just touching the water, move the pen across the surface of the water. See if you can make a line of bubbles. Making big and long lines of bubbles, see if you can write your name.

SOAPY WATER IN PAN

A Spinning Top That Writes

There are all sorts of spinning tops. Some make sounds as they spin. Others change colors as they move at different speeds. Have you ever seen one that writes as it spins around?

YOU WILL NEED:

  1 ball-point pen, or a felt-tip pen
  3 plastic lids: one large lid as on a plastic ice cream container, and two smaller lids as on margarine containers
  1 top part of a dishwashing soap bottle

CUT HERE→

NEW

HOW TO DO IT:

  1. With a knife, cut off the part of the soap container on which the top is screwed.
  2. Unscrew the top piece. You will now have two pieces as shown.

A   B

3. Next, find the center of each of the lids. Some lids already have a small dimple or mark exactly in the center. If you need to find the center, a quick way is shown in the drawing below: find the point on the lid that will let the lid balance.

4. Cut a hole in the center of one smaller lid. Make the hole large enough so that part B of the container top will slide through but will still fit snugly.

THE LID WILL BALANCE
WHEN YOU FIND THE
CENTER.

5. Do the same for the large lid, then the other smaller lid until top B goes through the three lids as shown below and fits snugly.

6. Before screwing top A onto top B, take the cap off top A and remove the crosspiece from inside the stem of top A.

7. After screwing top A onto top B, put a pen through the hole in A as shown in the drawing below. Be sure to replace the cap.

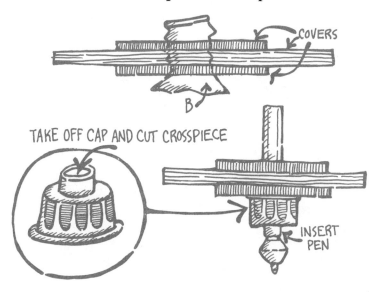

COVERS

B

TAKE OFF CAP AND CUT CROSSPIECE

INSERT PEN

8. From a wooden pencil, cut four or five pieces about one-half inch in length.

9. Place these pieces of wood inside the part between the wall and the pen. You may have to shave the side of each piece of wood to get a better fit. You want the pen to fit so snugly that it will not pop out when you are drawing on paper.

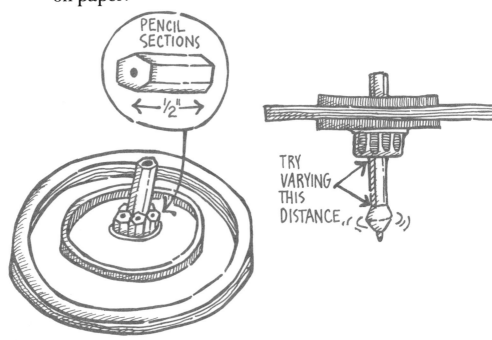

PENCIL SECTIONS

←—½"—→

TRY VARYING THIS DISTANCE.

One way to get a good spin is to hold the pen in hand as shown on the right. When the top is spinning, look below the lid and watch what the tip of the pen is doing. The pen should be making different kinds of circular designs such as those shown below.

As you get better at spinning the top and making a design, try changing the position of the different parts of the top. See how changing the position of the yellow cap or moving the lids up and down the pen will affect the designs you can make.

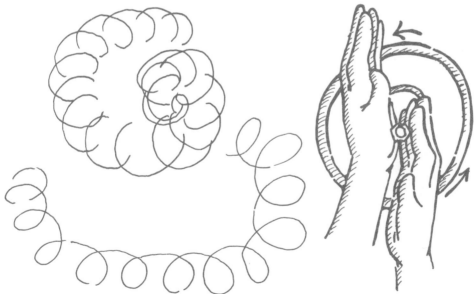

THE END?

This book stops here, but there are still more investigations you can do with ball-point pens. As you now can see, the pen and its parts can be used to make all sorts of things. Keep parts of ball-point pens around, and try using them for fun and learning.